SELF MANTRA

A GUIDE FOR SUCCESSFUL LIFE

VENKAT SURESH

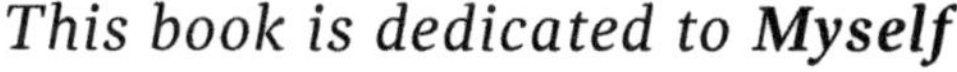

*This book is dedicated to **Myself***

&

To **MyExperiences** that helped me to keep this book physcially handy.

Contents

Contents

Foreword

Here My name is "EXPERIENCE" I am the authors internal voice of thoughts, I shared several facts and information to the author in Journey of his life and work, all together I am very happy that he Introduced this book to all of you, and you are at the right page, you had took a right book to change your lifes. I feel that Following the words in the book can help you as a torch in the dark when you are facing problems. Again I thank each and everyone who took this book, also if they adopt the mantra's they can have best results in their life...

All the very best to all of you and good luck Dear Venkat Suresh for this effort and works for people. ANy one person if changed through this book will change the lifes of millions of people...

Foreword

Preface

My one and only intention is to help people to get out of their miseries and stress. By using this book one can plan to move forward from where they stopped. Also it is very important that By reading or reciting the facts in this book as mentioned one can make things as Habits after several days of practice one can easily adopt the changes that are necessary to be successful in life.

Preface

Acknowledgements

I thank Myself and Myexperiences for this effort and support. Also Publishing partner to make this possible from printing this book out of letters.

Prologue

Always follow these rules when you start reading this book.

- Understand the concept as it is stright forwarded in nature you need to understand the depth of the concept with your though process.
- Don't read when you are emotionally disturbed instead Read this Book to avoid emotional disturbances.
- Read every day once all these 18 Mantra's whcich helps you to stay focussed.
- We also attached PLANNERS to help you in your process.
- One thing You need to remember is You must be commited to your Goal and works to get fullfillment in life.
- Texts In **BOLD** must be memorized in your day to day activites so that you try to aviod or come out problems
- For Interaction I had provided Planners and To Do list to interactively implement your goals.

CHAPTER ONE

Rule Your Time That Shapes Your Life

Rule your time handle it carefully, it has the power to shape or destroy your life plans, the only weapon you have is, just always say to yourself,

"This is My time and the only time I had with me is Now, I am going to utilize it to bring the best out of Me"

Do this regularly that it will become a Habit for you.

Always remember Time is the tool that helps you to get Treasures in life use this wisely.

ALWAYS MAKE A TASK SCHEDULAR FOR BEST TRACKING OF YOUR TIME.

CHAPTER TWO

You are the Ultimate Dictator for your life make it glorious.

You are the ultimate Dictator for your life make it glorious and fulfill your life on this planet, Life you are leading with out your control is an ordinary thing that most of the people face. But if you have command on decisions, work, people, questioning others for right will take you to the next level of extraordinary person. Always remember in mind i.e.

"I am the Dictator of my Life, I will think wisely, I will act Wisely, I will plan Wisely, I will oppose Wisely, I can change the circumstances, I had everything in me to change Everything."

Do this regularly that it will become a Habit for you. Always remember You are only You who can help You out to get out from Worse.

ALWAYS OPEN TO DISCUSSIONS WHERE MIXED VIEWS EVOLVE, SO THAT IN GROUP YOU TRY TO CONVINCE YOUR THOUGHTS WISELY.

CHAPTER THREE

Learn New Things

Before influencing others first acquire the knowledge that supports or smoothen the process, as a lubricant for a machine to work properly, like wise knowledge will function as a lubricant for your thought machines work and execute properly. Pick a best source that enlighten your process.

"I always learn New Things by Reading/ Observing to update my focus & Views."

Do this regularly that it will become a Habit for you.

Always remember that a smart gadget needs to be update in terms of software to work properly, like wise learning new things can update your thoughts to achieve the maximum of your process.

TRY TO READ OR LISTEN OR OBSERVE WITH OPEN MIND WITHOUT ANY DEVIATIONS. BE CALM & FOCUSED WHILE DOING THIS, DON'T DISTRACT.

CHAPTER FOUR

Use Digital World Work for You

Always do not fall in the trap of digital world, which makes you as a tool for their revenue, instead use digital world works for you to generate **Leads or Resource** for your Process.

"I always utilize each and every opportunity in the digital world for welfare and development of my process, I don't distract the ideology by getting into the digital mania distractions, I will utilize all the resources available in the digital world to enhance or level up my process."

Do this regularly that it will become a Habit for you.

Always remember that every objective will have a two-faced fact One is Positive side and other is negative side, you need to identify the real side of the digital world that helps you as a **TROJON HORSE** in **Trojon War.**

TRY TO LEARN NEW WAYS THAT HELPS YOU TO MASTER UTILIZATION OF DIGITAL WORLD TO LEVEL-UP YOUR PROCESS.

CHAPTER FIVE

Grab Power of Situation & Cash-Out

Always have power to cash out any situation that enables you to reach the goal of fulfillment in your process. Always try to highlight that the decision is within your hands & control. And you are the decision maker even the process is extremely hard to evaluate. It can give you a chance to analyze the difficulty, and to decide.

"I always utilize each and every opportunity or situation that helps me to move further in the process of my goals, whatever however wherever I will grab & I can Grab situation into my control."

Do this regularly that it will become a Habit for you.

Always remember situation is a key for your success, it may be a business, job, education, house making whatever, but the right time to do is very crucial and that should be utilized wisely.

TRY TO LEARN NEW WAYS THAT HELPS YOU TO MASTER UTILIZATION OF SITUATION. COMEOUT FO THE BOX TO DO THIS.

CHAPTER SIX

Destination of Tressure is Always an Up & Down

You know one thing people who are successful had more painful stories back in their life, there may be Wrong decisions, lack of opportunity, discrimination, discourage, political factors it may be in family or society or the nation several factors influence, these are Up's & Down's, but developing and getting success beyond that is the 1% successful people are doing. Tressures will only live with successful people, the Tressure of **HAPPINESS** to Health, Wealth, Power.

"I always object the negative impacts that my surroundings influence on my decision and process, I am one who can only effect my life routine & decision if I get into this trap of oppression."

Do this regularly that it will become a Habit for you.

Always try to identify the process that gives a clear picture of upcoming Up or Down sides of the road to the process.

TRY TO IMPROVE OBSERVATION SKILLS THAT ARE KEY TO BECOME INFLUENCER IN LIFE.

CHAPTER SEVEN

Always accept Experiences from Failure

Failures can give us a clear picture of what decision that we had taken in the past influenced to get failed, from that we can have an opportunity to change the plan that we are executing based on that decision. Failure can revamp the process to ultimate glory of success.

"I always accept failure as a precious one that helps me to get out of the worse to the best of my life, I always learn from failures and revamp the plans based on the results of the failure"

Do this regularly that it will become a Habit for you.

A failure in my sense is a great teacher or influencer who can shape your life to the ultimate level of success if you utilize it properly.

FAILURE IS THE GOLDEN STATE OF SUCCESS
THE PRICELESS STATE.

CHAPTER EIGHT

Avoid Past Memories to see Rapid Growth progress.

Memories are quite different from experiences we can accept experiences, but we need to avoid memories as they may guide you to wrong ways through Emotional thoughts which disturbs the process that is ongoing, it will affect your logical decision-making ability. Do not get into this trap from your brain.

“I always object memories that impact my logical decision-making ability that distracts my process. I am the commandant of My life.”

Do this regularly that it will become a Habit for you.

When it comes to life both emotional & logical thought processes will play vital role, but Logical thought process can avoid you from maximum failures and can save more time to achieve your process.

TRY TO DISTRACT FROM DISCUSSIONS OR WORDS THAT EFFECTS YOUR LOGICAL DECISION MAKING THROUGH EMOTIONS.

CHAPTER NINE

Do not let anyone interfere with your Life

General Psychological facts of most commonly people try to interfere in others works or life this can make a situation better or bitter, so always try to identify the intentions of the person who are interfering in your life, avoid them if their words are harming or influencing your ideology in the process. Do not panic just ask them to get out off from the place of your sight.

"I oppose who interfere in my life and decisions who disturbs my plan, I strictly tell them to get out of from the place of my sight."

When it comes to the above situation my Suggestion to you is think from the other persons scenario, then you can be able to understand the intension of the other person. Here the important thing is You should not interfere with Emotional Decisions where they impact the situation into drastic way.

THINK WISELY NOT EMOTIONALLY TO GET OUTOFF THE SITUATION.

CHAPTER TEN

Always Love Yourself First Then Others Next

Some people always degrade or downgrade themselves think that they cannot fit for anything, but they are willing to do. They are rapidly influenced by the society he is around. gradually loses control and it may lead sometimes to terrible decisions. So, to overcome this always Love Yourself First.

"I LOVE MYSELF."

Do this regularly that it will become a Habit for you.

First self-love is particularly important when it comes to you and your family, you should have a clear idea about yourself. What you can and cannot do only comes from understanding your potential, which comes from observation, and without self-love it cannot be achieved because you do not want to love yourself first.

LOVE YOURSELF FRIST THAT'S THE FIRST STEP OF YOUR SUCCESS.

CHAPTER ELEVEN

Have clear Vision & Mission

Always have a vision followed with a mission which will help you to get clear Idea about your destination of your journey. Vision should impact the mission which in turn Impact Life and process of work.

"I HAD A VISION & MISSION WHICH I ACHIVE & REACH MY GOAL."

Do this regularly that it will become a Habit for you.

Vision is the primary Ideation of Goal, where it transforms to mission by adding tasks to the vision, which in return will update you to the next level. Trust the process so that the vision and mission can be achieved.

VISION & MISSION WITH AMBITION CAN FORM A TRANSMISSION TO NEXT LEVEL.

CHAPTER TWELVE

Have Commitment To your Goals

Always have commitment and be committed to what you are doing to achieve progress. Things take time to achieve, in meanwhile we can feel failing, and drawback from the works can influence our thoughts to withdraw our efforts, this is the right time to motivate yourself and transform your infusion of efforts in it. Everything is possible in this world nothing is impossible for you.

"I CAN DO ANYTHING EVERYTHING IS POSSIBLE FOR ME BY ME TO ME."

Do this regularly that it will become a Habit for you.

Vision is the primary Ideation of Goal, where it transforms to mission by adding tasks to the vision, which in return will update you to the next level. Trust the process so that the vision and mission can be achieved.

ANYTHING EVERYTHING CAN BE AQUIRED BY YOU ONE THING SHOULD HAVE IS COMMITMENT TO YOURSELF.

CHAPTER THIRTEEN

Hatters Hate only when you are Growing

Haters are the indication of your progress, more the hatters it shows that you are rapidly growing to your destination. But be cautious to all such people as they always show the way and distracts us and wastes time and effort of your work.

"HATER'S WILL BE HATTER'S DOER'S WILL BE DOER'S, I AM DOER I WILL DO ANYTHING AND CAN DO ANYTHING."

Do this regularly that it will become a Habit for you.

Haters spend time analyzing our activities, but we need to do our work and speed up our efforts that they cannot even reach your thoughts. So always do the right things that can support your progress.

HATERS DO THEIR JOB WHICH WAS GIVEN BY DOERS TO DO, THAT'S HOW HATERS DO WITHOUT TAKING ANY SALARY FROM US.

CHAPTER FOURTEEN

Respect Every Earning You Made in the Process

It may be a penny or rupee, but it should be respected. There are two sides of living lives one side people are concentrated for money and physical assets on the other end peace, happiness etc. will come. But money is the fuel for this Era. I always suggest you all to respect Money and Its derivatives.

"I WILL RESPECT MONEY AND DERIVATIVES FROM IT, AND I HAVE SURPLUS EVEN IN HARDTIMES."

Do this regularly that it will become a Habit for you. Money is the God and there is a huge amount in circulation. According to 2022 stats There is approximately US$ 40 trillion in circulation: this includes all the physical money and the money deposited in savings and checking accounts. Money in the form of investments, derivatives, and cryptocurrencies exceeds $1.3 quadrillion.

GRAB YOUR PORTION IN THIS CAKE BUDDY

WORLD TODAY IS HELPING PEOPLE EACH OTHER NOT FOR ETHICAL VALUES BUT FOR MONEY, THE ULTIMATE GOAL TO EACH AND EVERYONE WHO ARE HERE, EVEN YOU AND ME.

CHAPTER FIFTEEN

Update yourself based on Society Needs to Survive

Update yourself and your business or work based on the society movement towards new things which helps you to survive and sustain to keep your assets and revenues stable.

"I WORK BASED ON TRAITS AND NEEDS IN THE SOCIETY, I ACHIEVE IT, I ACQUIRE IT."

Update your business, Life, Work, Style, Passions, Visions, Missions, all around 360° to survive in this world.

CHAPTER SIXTEEN

Kill Fear with Perfection in Your Commitment

Fear comes when you feel insecure, generally people feel insecure when they don't have any possession or standard money flow if it is a business, family, friends, peer groups, and many more in all these the only thing you feel in insecure or not perfect, so my suggestion is to Create yourself bound to commitment which in turn will give you perfection and result. Where we do not have a place for

FEAR

"I AM THE RIGHT PERSON TO KILL FEAR AND MAKE PEOPLE COME OUT OF IT."

Do this regularly that it will become a Habit for you.

Perfection can kill all the disabilities of our life mentally. Being mentally fit is the first fore most to grab anything into your hands. I suggest you take an Oath that I will commit to myself for my growth.

WORLD HAS FULL OF OPPURTUNITIES AND ITS YOUR TIME TO OCCUPY THE POSITION IT MADE FOR YOU MY DEAR CHOOSE WISELY WITH SMILE AND

POSITIVITY.

CHAPTER SEVENTEEN

Be Bold

"BOLD"

Always be bold and face any situation and question from coward people who feel that they know everything. Instead of Arguing Just be Bold to all such persons in your life.

"I AM BOLD ENOUGH THAT I CAN DO ANYTHING THAT I WISH TO DO."

Do this regularly that it will become a Habit for you.

Being bold is not a matter but in the matter of emotions again you must be cautious. Emotions always makes you deaf and dumb which is far more dangerous that being silent.

BOLD – BOLD - BOLD

TO BE IN PLACE **1** YOU MUST PUSH BACK ALL THE AFTER NUMBERS OF **1** WHICH NEEDS BOLDNESS AND COURAGE TO DO SO. IMPROVE SUCH TRIATS IN YOUR LIFE WHICH HELPS YOU BUILD AN EMPIRE OF RICHES...

CHAPTER EIGHTEEN

You are the Warrior, and you can do Anything

As a Warrior you mush fight for your life if you delay a minute someone in this world will occupy the place and rule you under their leadership.

"I AM THE WARRIOR FOR MY LIFE, I WILL FIGHT AND ACHIEVE EVRYTHING I WANT."

Do this regularly that it will become a Habit for you.

People only follow but ruler rules the people who they follow him. So here the context is you must be a Yoda for your whole life to transform your life. I suggest that be peaceful, strong, courage, stress free.

WORLD WILL BOWDOWM TO WHOM SHOWS COURAGE, AND STRONG.

CHAPTER NINETEEN

Planners

We are adding feature of 1 Year planner and other helpful planners to track your updates.

January

Monthly Planner

Month: ____ **Year:** ____

MON	TUE	WED	THU	FRI	SAT	SUN

To Do List

- ○ ....
- ○ ....
- ○ ....
- ○ ....
- ○ ....
- ○ ....
- ○ ....
- ○ ....

Goals

- ○ ....
- ○ ....
- ○ ....

February

Monthly Planner

Month: Year:

MON	TUE	WED	THU	FRI	SAT	SUN

To Do List

- ○ ....
- ○ ....
- ○ ....
- ○ ....
- ○ ....
- ○ ....
- ○ ....
- ○ ....

Goals

- ○ ....
- ○ ....
- ○ ....

March

Monthly Planner

Month: ______ **Year:** ______

MON	TUE	WED	THU	FRI	SAT	SUN

To Do List

- ○ ....
- ○ ....
- ○ ....
- ○ ....
- ○ ....
- ○ ....
- ○ ....
- ○ ....

Goals

- ○ ....
- ○ ....
- ○ ....

April

Monthly Planner

Month: ______ **Year:** ______

MON	TUE	WED	THU	FRI	SAT	SUN

To Do List

- ○ ....
- ○ ....
- ○ ....
- ○ ....
- ○ ....
- ○ ....
- ○ ....
- ○ ....

Goals

- ○ ....
- ○ ....
- ○ ....

May

Monthly Planner

Month: ______ Year: ______

MON	TUE	WED	THU	FRI	SAT	SUN

To Do List

- ○ ....
- ○ ....
- ○ ....
- ○ ....
- ○ ....
- ○ ....
- ○ ....
- ○ ....

Goals

- ○ ....
- ○ ....
- ○ ....

June

Monthly Planner

Month: ______ **Year:** ______

MON	TUE	WED	THU	FRI	SAT	SUN

To Do List

- ○ ....
- ○ ....
- ○ ....
- ○ ....
- ○ ....
- ○ ....
- ○ ....
- ○ ....

Goals

- ○ ....
- ○ ....
- ○ ....

July

Monthly Planner

Month: ______ **Year:** ______

MON	TUE	WED	THU	FRI	SAT	SUN

To Do List

- ○ ....
- ○ ....
- ○ ....
- ○ ....
- ○ ....
- ○ ....
- ○ ....
- ○ ....

Goals

- ○ ....
- ○ ....
- ○ ....

August

Monthly Planner

Month: ______ Year: ______

MON	TUE	WED	THU	FRI	SAT	SUN

To Do List

- ○ ....
- ○ ....
- ○ ....
- ○ ....
- ○ ....
- ○ ....
- ○ ....
- ○ ....

Goals

- ○ ....
- ○ ....
- ○ ....

September

Monthly Planner

Month: ______ Year: ______

MON	TUE	WED	THU	FRI	SAT	SUN

To Do List

- ○ ....
- ○ ....
- ○ ....
- ○ ....
- ○ ....
- ○ ....
- ○ ....
- ○ ....

Goals

- ○ ....
- ○ ....
- ○ ....

October

Monthly Planner

Month: ______ Year: ______

MON	TUE	WED	THU	FRI	SAT	SUN

To Do List

- ○ ....
- ○ ....
- ○ ....
- ○ ....
- ○ ....
- ○ ....
- ○ ....
- ○ ....

Goals

- ○ ....
- ○ ....
- ○ ....

November

Monthly Planner

Month: ______ Year: ______

MON	TUE	WED	THU	FRI	SAT	SUN

To Do List

- ○ ....
- ○ ....
- ○ ....
- ○ ....
- ○ ....
- ○ ....
- ○ ....
- ○ ....

Goals

- ○ ....
- ○ ....
- ○ ....

December

Monthly Planner

Month: ____ **Year:** ____

MON	TUE	WED	THU	FRI	SAT	SUN

To Do List

- ○ ....
- ○ ....
- ○ ....
- ○ ....
- ○ ....
- ○ ....
- ○ ....
- ○ ....

Goals

- ○ ....
- ○ ....
- ○ ....

To Do List

TO - DO LIST

- ■
- ■
- ■
- ■
- ■
- ■
- ■
- ■
- ■
- ■
- ■
- ■
- ■

To Do List

TO - DO LIST

- ■
- ■
- ■
- ■
- ■
- ■
- ■
- ■
- ■
- ■
- ■
- ■
- ■

To Do List

TO - DO LIST

- ■
- ■
- ■
- ■
- ■
- ■
- ■
- ■
- ■
- ■
- ■
- ■
- ■

To Do List

TO - DO LIST

■

■

■

■

■

■

■

■

■

■

■

■

■

CHAPTER TWENTY

My Mindful Planner

Enter Caption

Hope For Your Change

Finally we hope for a change in your life.

Printed by Libri Plureos GmbH in Hamburg,
Germany